Doing Your Best

Kimberley Jane Pryor

 **Marshall Cavendish**
Benchmark
New York

This edition first published in 2011 in the United States of America by Marshall Cavendish Benchmark
An imprint of Marshall Cavendish Corporation
All rights reserved.

Website: www.marshallcavendish.us

This publication represents the opinions and views of the author based on Kimberley Jane Pryor's personal experience, knowledge, and research. The information in this book serves as a general guide only. The author and publisher have used their best efforts in preparing this book and disclaim liability rising directly and indirectly from the use and application of this book.

Other Marshall Cavendish Offices: Marshall Cavendish International (Asia) Private Limited, 1 New Industrial Road, Singapore 536196 • Marshall Cavendish International (Thailand) Co Ltd. 253 Asoke, 12th Flr, Sukhumvit 21 Road, Klongtoey Nua, Wattana, Bangkok 10110, Thailand • Marshall Cavendish (Malaysia) Sdn Bhd, Times Subang, Lot 46, Subang Hi-Tech Industrial Park, Batu Tiga, 40000 Shah Alam, Selangor Darul Ehsan, Malaysia

Marshall Cavendish is a trademark of Times Publishing Limited

All websites were available and accurate when this book was sent to press.

Library of Congress Cataloging-in-Publication Data

Pryor, Kimberley Jane.
    Doing your best / Kimberley Jane Pryor.
        p. cm. — (Values)
    Includes index.
    Summary: "Discusses what values are and how doing your best can help you"—Provided by publisher.
    ISBN 978-1-60870-142-1
    1. Excellence—Juvenile literature. 2. Virtues—Juvenile literature. 3. Values—Juvenile literature.
    4. Children—Conduct of life— Juvenile literature. I. Title.
    BJ1533.E82P79 2011
    179'.9—dc22

                                                                        2009042677

First published in 2010 by
MACMILLAN EDUCATION AUSTRALIA PTY LTD
15–19 Claremont Street, South Yarra 3141

Visit our website at www.macmillan.com.au or go directly to www.macmillanlibrary.com.au

Associated companies and representatives throughout the world.

Managing Editor: Vanessa Lanaway
Editor: Helena Newton
Proofreader: Kirstie Innes-Will
Designer: Kerri Wilson
Page layout: Pier Vido
Photo researcher: Sarah Johnson (management: Debbie Gallagher)
Production Controller: Vanessa Johnson

Printed in China

Acknowledgments
The author and the publisher are grateful to the following for permission to reproduce copyright material:

Front cover photograph: Schoolgirl raising her hand, Digital Vision/Getty Images

Photos courtesy of:
© Moodboard/Corbis, 4; Blue jean images/Getty Images, 28; Philip J Brittan/Getty Images, 26; Jeff Cadge/Getty Images, 29; Digital Vision/Getty Images, 1; DreamPictures/Vstock/Getty Images, 13; Frank Gaglione/Getty Images, 24; GeoStock/Getty Images, 16; Sean Justice/Getty Images, 7; Wang Leng/ Getty Images, 5; Didier Robcis/Getty Images, 22; Steve Teague/Getty Images, 6; © Carmen Martínez Banús/iStockphoto, 14; © Jane norton/iStockphoto, 20; Jupiter Unlimited, 9, 10, 21; Charlie Abad/Photolibrary, 15; Birgid Allig/Photolibrary, 17; Bill Bachmann/Photolibrary, 23; David 4X5 Coll-Harrigan/ Photolibrary, 19; Jupiter Images/Photolibrary, 27; Monkey Business Images Ltd/Photolibrary, 8; © Sergey Petrov/Shutterstock, 30; Stockxpert, 3, 11, 12, 18, 25.

While every care has been taken to trace and acknowledge copyright, the publisher tenders their apologies for any accidental infringement where copyright has proved untraceable. Where the attempt has been unsuccessful, the publisher welcomes information that would redress the situation.

For Nick, Ashley, and Thomas

135642

Contents

When a word is printed in **bold**, you can look up its meaning in the Glossary on page 31.

Values

Values are the things you believe in. They guide the way:

- you think
- you speak
- you **behave**

Values help you to behave well when you travel on a bus.

Values help you to decide what is right and what is wrong. They also help you to live your life in a **meaningful** way.

Values help you to follow the rules when playing chess.

Doing Your Best

Doing your best is trying as hard as you can to do things well. It is paying attention when you do activities or jobs.

It is important to pay attention when you clean your pet's cage.

Doing your best is also finding out what you are good at and what you enjoy doing. It is trying to develop your special **skills**.

People who enjoy riding bicycles will improve if they practice their riding skills.

People Who Do Their Best

People who do their best do more than they need to. They put in extra **effort** when they do activities or jobs. They also spend extra time on them if they can.

The more effort you put into your school science project, the better your project will be.

People who do their best find ways to enjoy what they are doing. They work cheerfully with their family, friends, and neighbors.

Cooking can be fun if you do your best to help.

Doing Your Best with Family

You can do your best with family by being careful when doing jobs at home. This means being careful when you do little jobs and when you do big jobs.

Family members can do their best by being careful when working together in the garden.

You can also do your best with family by doing one job at a time. This means giving a job your full attention and working steadily until you finish.

It is important to pay attention when you clean the table.

Doing Your Best with Friends

Being **creative** is one way to do your best with friends. You can be creative by making up new games with friends. You can write stories and draw pictures together.

Creative people sometimes decorate a birthday cake for a friend.

Helping animals is another way to do your best with friends. Some friends work together to make ponds for frogs or to build houses for birds.

Friends who find a frog inside a house can place it carefully back outside.

Doing Your Best with Neighbors

Doing your best with neighbors means being **tolerant**. It means trying not to upset or disturb your neighbors. It also means apologizing to your neighbors when you need to.

Forgiving your neighbors if their new puppy howls shows tolerance.

Another way to do your best is to help make your neighborhood a safer place. You could talk to your teacher if you think your school needs better **pedestrian** crossings.

People need pedestrian crossings in their neighborhoods to help them cross roads safely.

Ways To Do Your Best

There are many different ways to do your best with your family, friends, and neighbors. Being **prepared** is a good way to start doing your best.

You can prepare to build with construction toys by listening to a friend's instructions.

Being **organized** will help you to do your best.
Persevering and practicing are also part of doing
your best.

If you persevere, you
will be able to finish a
difficult jigsaw puzzle.

Being Prepared

Being prepared is one way to do your best.
People who are prepared read or listen to instructions before starting an activity or a job.

If you listen to instructions, you will learn how to snorkel safely.

People who are prepared also get everything they need before starting an activity or job. They know that this will help them to do the activity or the job correctly.

You can prepare to paint by getting your paper, paint, and paintbrushes ready.

Being Organized

Being organized is another way to do your best. Organized people know what they need to do and when they need to do it.

Making a list of what you need to do will help you to be organized.

People who are organized can find what they need when they need it. They give each thing its own place. They put things away when they finish using them.

Folding your clean clothes before putting them away will help you to stay organized.

Pacing Yourself

Pacing yourself helps you to do your best. If you have enough time for a job, you are more likely to do it well.

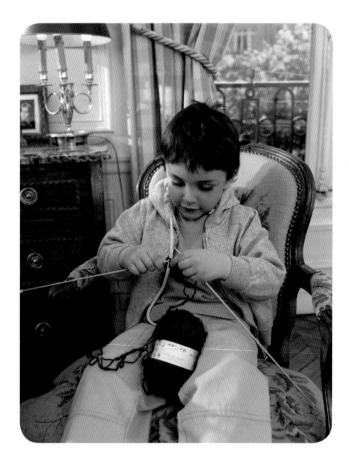

You will be able to knit well if you take your time.

Some jobs are difficult or can take a lot of time to do. You may find it helpful to take regular breaks to eat, drink, or exercise.

Taking regular breaks when making a model ship will give you energy to keep working.

Persevering

Persevering is part of doing your best. People who persevere try to finish what they start. They keep trying even when a job is difficult or takes a long time.

Climbers who persevere eventually reach the top of the wall.

People who persevere also keep trying when **obstacles** stand in their way. They think of ways to **solve problems** and do not give up easily.

Getting up and trying to ice skate again after falling shows perseverance.

Practicing

Practicing sports and hobbies will help you to do your best. People can go to lessons or classes to learn new skills. Practicing helps people improve these skills.

If you practice doing karate, your kicks will improve.

People who want to be good at playing musical instruments can take lessons. They often learn new pieces of music during lessons. Then they practice alone or with others.

It is fun to practice playing a musical instrument with a friend.

Behaving Well

Behaving well allows you to do your best. Listening when other people offer advice is one way to behave well. You will learn different things from different teachers and coaches.

If you listen to your art teacher, you may learn how to make origami birds.

Being a good sport is another way to behave well. You will have more fun if you **cooperate** with the referee and other players.

Cooperating with the referee during a soccer game shows that you are a good sport.

Personal Set of Values

There are many different values. Everyone has a personal set of values. This set of values guides people in big and little ways in their daily lives.

Ballet dancers do their best during performances.

Glossary

behave   Act in a certain way.

cooperate   Work together.

creative   Good at making or inventing things.

effort   Hard work.

meaningful   Important or valuable.

obstacles   Things that are in your way or that slow you down.

organized   Able to put things in order or arrange things neatly.

pedestrian   Going by foot.

persevering   Continuing to do something, often in spite of difficulties.

prepared   Ready.

problems   Things that are difficult to understand or do.

skills   Abilities that help you to do activities or jobs well.

solve   Find the answer to.

tolerant   Able to accept new and different ideas and ways of doing things.

Index